What to do of year

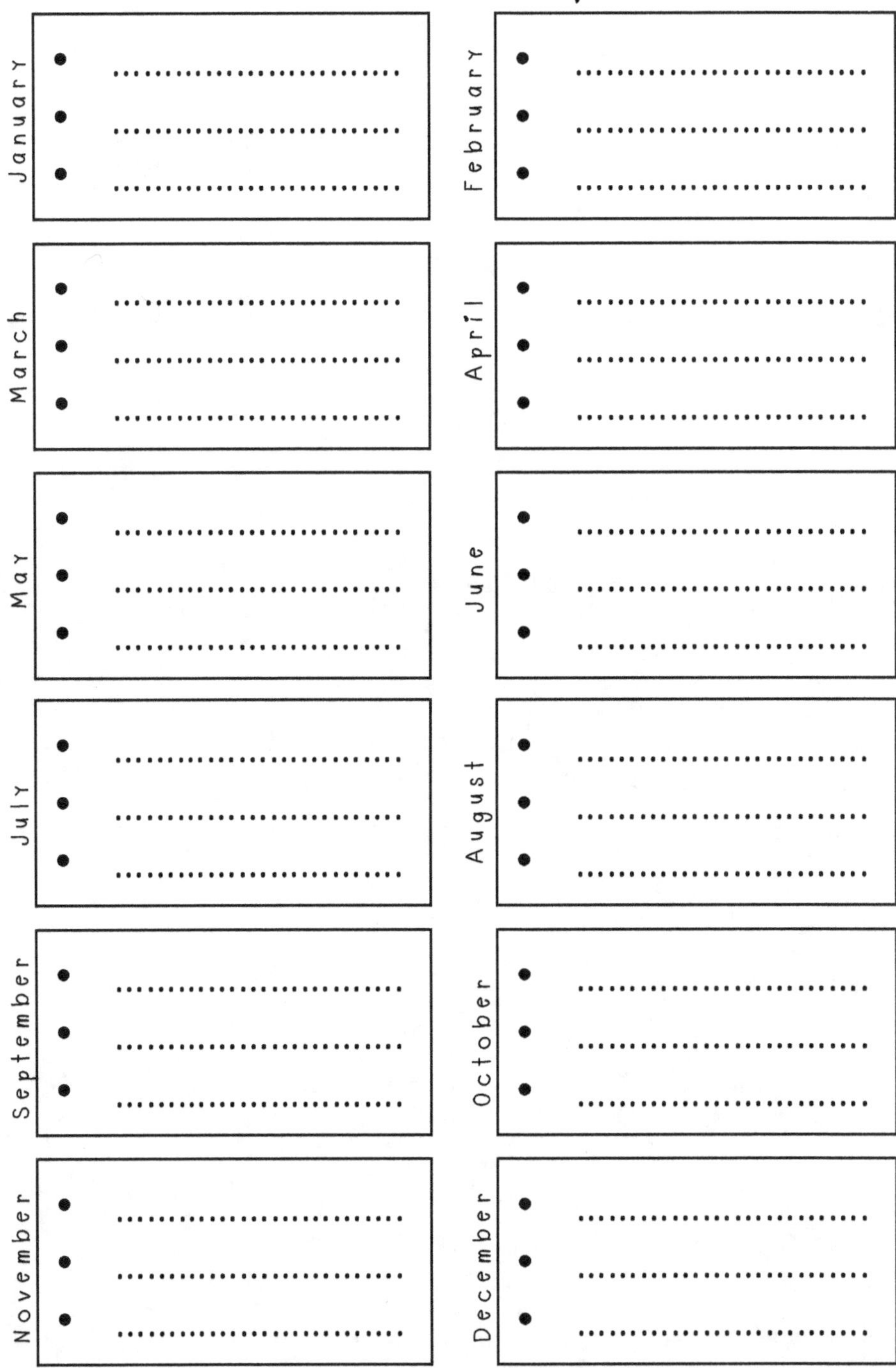

Question

Question...

....

....

....

Question

date
Question

Question……………………………………………………………………

Question..

Question..

Question..

Question...
....
....
....

Question...
....
....
....

Question...

Question

Question...

Question...
....
....
....

Question..
....
....
....

Question

date
Question

Question...

date
Question

date
Question

Question

Question..

....

Question...

....

Question

January

♡ **What to say**

....
....
....
....
....
....
....
....

♡ **What to say**

....
....
....
....
....
....
....
....

Question..

Question..

Question ....

Question

Question

Question

Question..

Question..

Question

date
Question

Question

Question..
....
....
....
....

Question

Question

Question..
....
....

date
Question

Question...

Question

Question……………………………………………………
…………………………………………………………………
…………………………………………………………………
…………………………………………………………………

Question

date
Question

February

♡ What to say

....
....
....
....
....
....
....
....

♡ What to say

....
....
....
....
....
....
....
....

Question...

Question

Question..

Question

Question..

....

Question...
....
....
....

Question

Question

Question

Question

Question...
....
....
....

date
Question

Question...

Question

Question

Question..

Question...
....
....
....

Question..

Question..
....
....
....

Question

Question..
....
....
....

Question

date
Question

Question

Question

date
Question

date
Question

Question..

....

....

....

date
Question

March

♡ **What to say**

....
....
....
....
....
....
....
....

♡ **What to say**

....
....
....
....
....
....
....
....

Question

Question..

Question...
....
....
....

Question

Question

Question...
....
....
....

Question

date
Question

Question.

Question...

....

Question

Question...
....
....
....
....

Question

Question...
....
....
....

Question

Question

Question

Question...

Question

Question

date
Question

date
Question

Question

April

♡ **What to say**

....
....
....
....
....
....
....
....

♡ **What to say**

....
....
....
....
....
....
....
....

Question..
....
....
....

Question..

....

Question..

Question...

Question

Question

Question..
....
                ....
                ....
                ....

Question..
....

date
Question

date
Question

Question..

Question

Question

Question..

Question

Question..

Question

Question..

Question..

Question

Question...

Question

date
Question

Question..
....
....
....

Question...

May

What to say

....

....

....

....

....

....

....

....

What to say

....

....

....

....

....

....

....

....

Question...
....
....
....

Question

date
Question

Question...
....
....
....

Question

Question..

Question ....

Question

Question

Question

Question

Question

date
Question

Question..
....

Question

Question

Question..

Question

Question..

Question

Question...

Question

Question..

....

Question..

June

♡ **What to say**

....
....
....
....
....
....
....
....

♡ **What to say**

....
....
....
....
....
....
....
....

Question...
....

Question...
....
....
....
....

Question...
....
....
....

Question..

....

Question

Question...
....
....
....

Question

Question

Question..

date
Question

Question..

Question...
....

Question

Question

Question..

....

date
Question

Question

Question

date
Question

date

Question

Question...
....
....

date
Question

July

♡ What to say

....
....
....
....
....
....
....
....

♡ What to say

....
....
....
....
....
....
....

Question

Question...

Question

Question..

....
....
....

Question

Question...
....
....
....

Question...
....
....
....
....

Question..

date
Question

Question...

Question

date
Question

Question.

Question

date
Question

date
Question

Question..
....
....
....

Question

Question..
....
....

date
Question

Question

date
Question

Question

Question...
....
....
....

Question

Question...
....
....
....

August

♡ What to say

....
....
....
....
....
....
....
....

♡ What to say

....
....
....
....
....
....
....
....

Question...
....
....
....

Question..

Question

date
Question

Question

Question..
....
....
....
....

Question

Question

Question

Question...
....

Question..
....
....
....

Question..
....
....
....

Question

Question

Question...
....
....
....

Question

Question...
....
....
....
....

Question

Question

September

♡ **What to say**

....
....
....
....
....
....
....
....

♡ **What to say**

....
....
....
....
....
....
....
....

Question

date
Question

Question..
....
....
....

date
Question

Question..

Question...

Question

Question..

....

Question...

Question...
....
....
....
....

Question..

....

date
Question

Question

Question

Question

date
Question

Question

Question

Question ....
....
....
....

Question

Question

Question

Question

Question

Question

Question

Question...
....

date

Question ....
....

Question

October

♡ What to say

....
....
....
....
....
....
....
....

♡ What to say

....
....
....
....
....
....
....
....

Question..
....
....
....

Question..

....

....

....

date
Question

Question..

....

....

date
Question

Question

Question...

Question...

....

Question

date
Question

Question..

Question...
....
....
....
....

Question

Question...
....
                    ....
                    ....

Question

Question...
....
....
....
....

Question..
....

Question..

Question

Question

Question

Question..

Question...

....

date Question..
....

Question

date
Question

November

♡ What to say

....
....
....
....
....
....
....
....

♡ What to say

....
....
....
....
....
....
....
....

Question

Question

Question...
....
....
....
....

Question

Question

date
Question

date
Question

Question..

date
Question

Question..

date
Question

Question

Question

Question..

Question

Question..

....

Question

date
Question

Question...
....
....
....
....

Question...
....
....

Question..

Question...

December

♡ What to say

....
....
....
....
....
....
....
....

♡ What to say

....
....
....
....
....
....
....
....

Note

www.ingramcontent.com/pod-product-compliance
Lightning Source LLC
Chambersburg PA
CBHW082333270726
48658CB00017B/2828